THE STACK
IS GETTIN

C000077546

THE STACK OF OWLS IS GETTING HIGHER

By Dawn Watson

THE EMMA PRESS

THE EMMA PRESS

First published in the UK in 2019 by the Emma Press Ltd

Poems copyright © Dawn Watson 2019

Edited by Richard O'Brien
Typeset by Emma Wright

ISBN 978-1-912915-33-0

A CIP catalogue record of this book
is available from the British Library.

Printed and bound in the UK
by Impact Print & Design, Hereford.

The Emma Press
theemmapress.com
hello@theemmapress.com
Birmingham, UK

CONTENTS

How To Kill Snakes with a Slipper

RED TOUCH BLACK, LUCKY JACK.
YELLOW ON RED, SOON BE DEAD
—US Deep South folk rhyme, 1862

She cuts the grass at the liquor store.
This is Pop Kola. This is Old Gold.
It's hard to see where the lawn ends
and the pine straw starts. Cypress plumb
the banks of the Ogeechee. Two nests
of longhorn crazy ants fight to the death.
Once, a copperhead fell from a branch
onto her head. Swirl of heavy rust
and lemon. She killed it with her slipper.
The clumped hanging moss is tickled
at the memory. The pitchfork shivers.
The oak hollow fills. The trout stand
to clap when the mower comes by.

Peach Season

after Simon Armitage

She vanished at twilight across the field, slipping
    to the woods
after clearing the leaves off the porch, leaving
    a note
for her wife and son and dismantling
    all the windows.
They had given her a basket and she filled it
    with peaches.
Hours passed, and she lost herself in peach trees.
    Then a day,
and she watched the orb spider knit
    a message
between two scuppernong vines. Then a month,
    and she took an axe,
made a pile of split wood. One night,
    she tucked
her wild legs beneath her and unscrewed
    them at the hip.

At home, her wife and son grew tired
    of magnolia cones
thumping the roof, and the air conditioning unit
    rattling the walls.
After a year, they scanned the fresh-cut field
    for a rare sight
of dolphins. The night was a closed box
    and they dug out

the recipe for peach pie. When the giant butterfly
  came clattering
up the hall, her wife could only freeze and hope
  it passed by.
Her son stretched out his arms to mimic
  the vast wingspan.
They puffed out their cheeks
  and laughed,
taking turns to bite the wooden spoon. At sunrise,
  the boy ran
a shower for his other mother and hoped
  she would reappear
in water the way sometimes the things we forget
  come back to us.

Years passed, and from the woods she watched
  lightning debunk
the boundary fence. The outhouse door
  walloped in the wind
and storms tore up the yellow field.
  When she didn't return,
her wife and son grew the peach trees higher
  and adjusted
the recipe to reduce the nutmeg. In October,
  the stars set fire
to the woodpile and cicadas clicked so loudly
  the peach stones broke.

The Boxer

I'm not a man at the weigh-in. I stuff
balled-up socks down my jocks
and clutch my breasts in fistfuls. You bet
I wear sharp shorts to a gun fight. I love
the cold eye iron, the Vaseline. They pack
my cut brow with flowers. I want to knock
you out the way the shop on Artillery Road
sells only hats and knives. I want to knock
you out like a careless wank. I'm not a man
when I land that peach of an uppercut. The ring
rope props your neck. The red corner squares
the towel. The referee waves it all off.

Yellow Punkins on the Oolenoy

'Pickens County was Cherokee Indian territory until the American Revolution'
—G. Anne Sheriff

The wind chimes are rusted, seven plumed bells.
Their stuck clappers hang in the back yard.
The black walnut tree is too stretched to seem gentle.
I pry one green fruit apart.
Its skin looks like a forest seen from a lighthouse.
My fingernails ring brown for weeks.
I sleep in a box at the top of the house.
The window overlooks the pet cemetery.
Its chipped glass rabbit guards the entrance.
I will not cross her.
Fire ants dance in outposts.
Fireflies clang their lights in flashes.
Tonight, there is blue fire in the eyes of coyotes at the treeline.
Racoons are a rumpus glow, the red eyes of deer drift sideways.
I sent for the wild boar yesterday.
The stack of owls is getting higher.
I am lit by seven hundred fires and want more.

All along the Oolenoy, yellow punkins stand like they walked there.
They are monstrously large and bloomed with rust.
William Sutherland has been dead for two hundred years.
That settler's son took a clutch night and made it afternoon.
He did always know how to twist a day along.
When I dislocated my collar bone, the doctor said:
Strange, it is easier to break a bone than force it out of place.
It was a lunar achievement.
The pioneers called this place Pumpkintown.
They had no ritual for spiny turtles.

River names tell the real stories.
The streams were green with change.
In Fall, the Oolenoy carries smoke and skeletons through my yard.
It yanked my mum from its spoondrift bank.
She was studying the light across wolves in June. I say all this to help you.
When the rains stop, I will plunder every one of those dumb punkins.
I'll carve jacks like in their teeth I see the moon.

Chicken Wings

I read God described as a bar of horizontal light, which makes sense: solid, angular radiance and geometric dependability. It's an image I can feel in my teeth; something I can get behind. I can run my tongue along its cool, hard ridges. I feel this way about chicken wings—but look, they're never right. If they have hot sauce, they're not crisp. If they are crisp, they've no blue cheese dip. If they have dip, there's no celery. I saw a woman with blue plasters on every fingertip eat chicken wings on the top deck of a London bus. I watched her rip and fling small bones. I almost cried, she was so determined. Near my stop, I told her, What we need is a horizontal bar of chicken wings, moulded stiff with celery, sauce and dip. She made an O with her mouth and agreed it would have solid, angular radiance and is something she could get behind.

Don't Shoot, Sir

On the North Poinsett Highway
in sleepy Travelers Rest
I made a left into a coffee house
when I should have given way.
A cop car squealed
into the parking lot. I switched off
the engine. He walked to my window
hand on gun.
I called him sir. He told me to get out.
Open the trunk. He said, Ma'am,
do you understand
I can shoot you and your son
and your wife and your brother
and his husband right here
in the parking lot.
The smell of coffee was distracting.
I said, Don't shoot, sir,
I am going to give you my shoes
and my laces if you want them.
The people watching
were yellow.
I said, Don't shoot, sir,
I am going to give you my black ice,
my dead flower drift,
my fat redbone coonhound.
The cop was a smoke trail.
I said, Don't shoot, sir,
forgive me, I will reach for my licence.

The trees were red lights
switched off and on
in the blue autumn.
The watching crowd ate
snow cones thoughtfully.
From a nest, the cop took a bird
and told me, Hold it.
I climbed into the car
with the bird in my hand
and it dashed. I cried
and said, I think this bird
is a gun,
and it dashed and dashed.

Bird on the School Path

There is this bird
furiously hoking
through the bushes
like *What.*
The fuck.
Is this leaf.
Doing. In my—
And this.
And fucking this.

Advice for Campers

1

Low clouds scuff the tips of oaks
edging the long field.

The border between our tents and yews

where sharp men with long ears,
tall women with crescent smiles
and string children with oranges for eyes
stand in the dark.

You squat in the toilet shack
lit by a hanging bulb.

2

Our eyes meet outside the kitchen.

3

Don't drink after six.
Pee your last before bed in your bag with a book
then your torch can stay on its hook

and what claws will be trees

and what ca-caws will be crows

and the bones gut-stretched by your tent when you rise
will be chitlins, friend. Jackrabbits.

At the Gas Station

The busted QT gas station is a wonderland.
It sells lost things. Look at the cuckoo spit,
maggots in a brown bag, black ice in the school yard,
Tybee Island skinny dips, unglued hugs.
Those pumps are full of sassafras and sweet bay,
one hundred shortleaf pines. You can fill your tank
with river birch. That motor oil is a just-new
strip mall in Athens. That gasoline is the advert
with the talking dog. That diesel is Elsie's barn,
mythic with honeysuckle. That mid-grade is how
to take a bath in a Spartanburg pond. This canopy
shelters truck stops, meat sticks, lottery tickets
and twenty-six flavours of slushy. You want advice?
Put the nozzle in your mouth and fill up.

We Can Chat About It by Teletext Which I Know Is Impossible

I'll ask on *page 3/88*
how your trip to Paris is going
and you'll reply with text updates
in 7-bit electronic code
with limited bandwidth.
So, by *page 13/88*
I'll know about your flight
and the landing, which was bu—
page 14/88
which was bumpy.
When you're at the canal
having hot dogs and fresh lemonade
I'll be on *page 26/88*
reading about your hotel check-in,
the difficulties with the bell boy
and how the lift smelled like f—
page 27/88
how the lift smelled like firelighters.
I'll ask about the Louvre
then on *page 39/88*
learn you switched rooms
since your girlfriend wanted a tower view
and your first room had no—
page 40/88
your first room had no window,
just a painting of a seagull in a scarf.
When you're grinning
at Montmartre,
wearing the sweater I gave you,
I'll be on *page 53/88*

13

catching up on the canal,
the hot dogs and fresh lemonade
and the prodigious number of—
page 54/88
The prodigious number of bridges.
I don't know.
Maybe I'll give up questions.
Just sit with the remote
eating Coco-Pops in the dark
reading about croissants,
walks by the Seine
and something about a ring,
textually garbled
and difficult to understand.
On *page 64/88*
I'll cave in and ask
are you happy?
Are you glad we're not friends?
Then wait through ten pages
of admittedly moving soliloquies
on Princess Diana's memorial
until *page 87/88*
when you'll reply, honestly, I—
page 88/88
you'll reply, honestly I—
and the doorbell will ring,
someone selling cookies,
and when I get back to the TV
it'll be on *page 2/88*
and I'll have to read again
how you got in your Volkswagen and—
page 3/88
got in your Volkswagen and left.

The M1 to Belfast

Do you remember the time I laughed at your dream? My hand on your leg
as you curled, a nervous driver, towards the plastic dash
and drove too fast at the line of hills separating the North from the South.
It's about here, every time, that the cummerbund M1 from Dublin

births lemon *Caution! Deer!* signs and snaps into a mountain, which in turn
erupts like a Coke float into the oak-flanked road to Belfast.
I always hope to catch the moment of transformation around some bend
in the road—beyond some wood where the hedges split

into fields and the fields squat into rocks and the rocks hoof into a mountain.
You were gripping the wheel with the sincere-but-distant expression
of someone listening to an earnest apology they can only partially hear
and I was watching for when the road turned into a mountain. Do you

remember you said your dad was wearing your socks when he shot your dog;
I laughed because I only heard the first bit, and realised too late
that the peaks had already woofed up from nowhere. Were you watching?
I complained, scanning the sudden valley. We missed it again.

Heading Home to East Tennessee via the Town of Bat Cave

Driving back from Greenville, fifty miles a long wait
for the Bat Cave sign on the interstate,
we pulled off to find
                                    there are no bats
and no caves for anyone looking. Slash pines stood

steep-banked in the foothills
                                    of Bluerock Mountain,
their bald peaks whipping
                                    and buckling like torn flags
as the heat rose bold through the valley.

I watched a hawk drift—wings tipped
                                    in a pike salute—
suddenly corkscrew loop to snatch up a jackrabbit
the colour of spat ink
like that sweet, fat hare weighed nothing at all.

We passed Wide River, neither wide
nor a river,

and in Johnson City, my mother-in-law turned
into a gas station to ask
                                    why I love horror films.

There was no gas in the pump, just peaches
in a barrel,
           like in *Rawhead Rex*, when a girl gripped
her boyfriend's hand as they ran for their lives
through the woods (she looked down
                              to find
it was literally just a hand she was holding).

I thought knowing horror might stop me
being devoured. It didn't,
                        and behind us a storm hung
ready to break
              over Bat Cave, which didn't need bats
or even caves to be Bat Cave,

and I thought of the soft body of the jackrabbit plucked
from its hopsage space suit,
from its pitch pine jackboots,
from the hot red bluffs
of the foothills with just a steam-whistle warning,
a thin *klee-uk*
              to cut the clear morning, which itself
was nothing but a small bush growing stars.

Non-Biological Motherhood in Euclidean Terms

I

In your first summer on earth,
a crow would perch on the roof
and watch me bottle-feed you in the yard.
It returned a piked caw for every kick and suck.
It would dive in a straight line
over the cracked concrete, gutter to gate,
and strike at the brass latch with its feet.
I think the crow was trying to let you out.
Is that ridiculous?

II

There's no such thing as a straight line.
Space is curved.
Straight lines are textbook concepts
that apply to Euclidean geometry.
The flat horizon is a circle.
In Euclid's first common notion, things equal
to the same thing are equal to each other.

III

Non-biological mothers from same-sex couples
are not equal to biological mothers
in emergency situations,
says the GP general manager. You see?
Doctors need to make snap judgements
and will struggle to draw a straight line
between you and your son.
You have different surnames.
You could be anyone.

The Sun is One Inch Above the Horizon

Sitting on the kerb at the Borstal,
the elders have the look of glass
diffused by sea gales. Crooked, tall
with elbows keen to quit the black morass
of picnic tables. They prowl the wall
of pointed stone, congregants bent
uncanny by salt winds underspent

on small red boats with axe flint sails.
The bruised mackerel sky
harbours runaways, twin vapour trails
threading blue like ley lines. I
watch the pale vines fade like tales
not mine to tell.
Not long 'til darkness falls

on Woburn House. It's carmine;
borscht in a white bowl through a screen door.
The sun is one inch above the horizon.
Tides froth as cormorants gore
the slanted shoreline.
I stack my half-torn books,
green corduroy trousers, a plastic chess rook,

Corn Flakes, old Nikes, a shoebox full
of peanut shells, ninety-one Beanos dried
brittle and buff, two rubbers, red wool
spooled and a well-worn Guide
to Ghosts. Black-head gulls
yawp on black rocks. I set a match
to it all. Limp tides snatch

the feet of kids on inflatable tyres sculled
with sticks, children
afloat where hope was hulled
and split. Long linden
shadows pull
light from roof balustrades
hung over sandcastles, spades

and yellow shell moulds. As the light
slips down the throat of the day—
a failed sun gobbled up tight
by the Irish Sea—the spray
is old Miss Clayton screaming right
in my face in P4. The salt
is the sting of my alkaline fault.

The gathering dark is the man
trailing me home from the shop
when I was nine—I ran
until I reached my gate to find him stopped
and watching from the road. The sand
is a thousand plastic splinters, pell-mell,
the day the gang broke our doorbell

prying it off with a butter knife.
They'd be back for the knocker.
The gull is Half Legs the dwarf
falling through our glass table, blocked
on vodka. The smoke is Bridget's hair
set on fire with a Berkeley Menthol.
I watched her lit from the hall.

They said kids cursed
the Borstal. It's the reverse.
Childhood draws the worst.
The shells are razed, the black rook bursts.
The trousers turn to ashes first.
The Corn Flakes glow white briefly.
The books are last to burn completely.

Hello, I Am Alive

Hello, I am alive,
although barely,
it feels. Often
I'm afraid of the dark,
but not tonight.

When I am afraid,
I see the girl
from The Exorcist
walking backwards
on fingers and toes

or standing beside me
with a very wide grin
when I roll over
in bed. In Los Angeles,
I jumped,

fully-clothed, into
a deep fountain;
my passport floated
up past my eyes.
When I was 23, I swore

I'd be dead at 24—
you see, I had
a colour dream
about my gravestone
back when dreams

seemed like powerful
launch pads.
Let's not forget,
losing a father
and sister to suicide

in Russian winter
led Pankejeff to dream
of white wolves
watching
from a walnut tree.

I was waiting for a bus
when a man asked
was there any chance
of a blowjob.
It was like

when fifteen wasps
got inside my shirt.
I stood by a bin
and they thought
I was a pineapple.

The fruit shop
has too many plums
to stack safely.
Are you a boy or a girl?
is the question

I was asked most
as a kid. I
was left-handed
until my teacher broke
his ruler on my desk

telling me to be
right-handed. I
kicked a boy
in the balls
when he wouldn't let me past

with my Coke.
I pushed a boy
into a hedge
when he wouldn't let me past
with my schoolbag. I

have genuinely
had enough
ham, I thought,
as I ate the ham
in silence.

Bird murmurations
are the closest thing
we have to magic
or the apocalypse.
I crashed

a snowmobile
into a tree
and white covered me
like a tonne blanket.
My mum shouted,

You're a lesbian.
I said, *I'm not*
but I was.
I am.
Fire is wildly

unbelievable
as a concept. I
don't know why
things take days to erupt
and sometimes years.

I am terrified
in case I go insane
and hurt people.
My favourite insult
is 'moon cat'.

I need to remind myself
things are solid.
This is a morgue chimney.
This is cold coffee.
These are train tracks.

That is a rope.
I was digging a plot
beside a warm army
of dock leaves
when a small boy

asked for more blue
for the sky.
I unravelled
all I could find.
We, in poetry,

has a reach.
We need monsters.
We are set on edge
by toes. We fear
strangers

taking our mushrooms
in the checkout line
like in Stephen King's *The Mist*.
I worry I have
my mother's hands.

There are many words
for light and death.
I am quick
to assume I'm wrong.
There is low grey cloud

on the light lines
as the train clicks
down to London.
I don't know
how to be okay

with dying. I can't
ride a horse. Oh,
let's just sit here
and look at this lake
for a while.

NOTES

In 'How to Kill Snakes with a Slipper', the Ogeechee is a 294-mile long blackwater river in the US state of Georgia.

'Peach Season' is after Simon Armitage's poem 'Gooseberry Season' from his collection *Kid*.

'Yellow Punkins on the Oolenoy' refers to the Oolenoy River. According to historian John Currahee, its name derives from *u'lana'wa*, the Cherokee name for the *Apalone spinifera* (a spiny, softshell turtle). A roadside historical marker in Pumpkintown (Pickens County, SC) reads: 'This community, settled before 1800, was named "Pumpkin Town" by an anonymous early traveler awed by the sight of the Oolenoy Valley covered with huge yellow pumpkins. The same tourists who visted nearby Table Rock Mtn. often stayed at William Sutherland's inn.'

In 'At the Gas Station', QT refers to the QuikTrip chain that operates across the South-Eastern United States.

In 'Advice for Campers', chitlins are a Deep South food made from cooked intestines.

In 'Heading Home to East Tennessee via the Town of Bat Cave', Bat Cave is a town in Henderson County, NC. It reportedly has North America's largest-known granite fissure cave. It is not open to the public.

ACKNOWLEDGEMENTS

Thanks are due to the journals in which some of these poems first appeared: *The Moth, The Manchester Review, Blackbird, The Open Ear,* and the *Poetry Ireland* ebook *Hello, I Am Alive* (2019). Thank you to Marty Cullen at BBC Arts Show X for recording 'Chicken Wings'.

I'm grateful to Emma Wright and my editor Richard O'Brien from The Emma Press, I cannot thank you both enough. Thank you to the Seamus Heaney Centre — in particular, to Stephen Sexton for his enthusiasm and care in helping develop these poems. Thank you to Conor Cleary for being the best pamphlet wingman I could hope for. Thanks to Doireann Ní Ghríofa for the support of both myself and the raging bird. Thanks to the very special Ashleigh Young.

Thank you to my brother James and sister Tanya, for everything. Thanks to Brendan Murphy, Deby McKnight, Mark Doty, Philippa Sitters, Stephani Dempsey, and all my family in America. Thank you to Doris Sinclair, always in the daffodils.

Above all, thank you to Sarah—there aren't enough thank yous. And to my son Art, here is a thank you as deep as the journey to the Underworld in Terraria hard mode.

ABOUT THE POET

Dawn Watson is a writer from Belfast. She is currently a PhD candidate at Queen's University, writing a prose poem novel and researching prose poetics. She worked as a sub editor in newspapers such as the *Sunday Times* in London, the *News of the World* in Dublin and the *Mirror* in Belfast.

She completed a Masters in Poetry at the Seamus Heaney Centre in 2018 after winning the Ruth West Poetry Scholarship. She was a 2018 Poetry Ireland Introductions Series poet and won the Doolin Writers' Poetry Award in the same year. Her writing has been published in journals including *The Manchester Review, Blackbox Manifold, The Stinging Fly, The Moth* and *The Tangerine*. She lives in Belfast with her wife, and has a son, Art.

ABOUT THE EMMA PRESS

The Emma Press is an independent publisher dedicated to producing beautiful, thought-provoking books. It was founded in 2012 by Emma Dai'an Wright in Winnersh, UK, and is now based in the Jewellery Quarter, Birmingham.

The Emma Press publishes poetry and fiction anthologies and pamphlets for adults and for children, with a growing list of translations.

The Emma Press has been shortlisted for the Michael Marks Award for Poetry Pamphlet Publishers in 2014, 2015, 2016 and 2018, winning in 2016.

theemmapress.com
emmavalleypress.blogspot.co.uk